Glimpses

by dsiii

© 2021 dsiii Publications

Daniel Salazar III
<u>Glimpses</u>
All rights reserved. No part of this publication may be reproduced, stored in a retrieval system or transmited in any form or by any means, electronic, mechanical, photocopying, recording or otherwise without the prior permision of the publisher or in accordance with the provisions of the Copyright, Designs and Patents Act 1988 or under the terms of any licence permitting limited copying issued by the Copyright Licensing Angency.

Published by: dsiii Publications

Text Design by: Daniel Salazar III

Cover Design by: Daniel Salazar III

A CIP record for this book is acailable from the Library of Congress Cataloging-in-Publication Data

ISBN-10: 1 30089 483 4

ISBN-13: 978 1 30089 483 4

Daniel Salazar III
GLIMPSES

dsiii Publications

"I am a continuous slow explosion of what we all are. Light. Energy. Love. Being. One. Nothing. Everything. No word exists for it. No sound. No smell. Nothing."

- dsiii

Splinters of Ice

Each of my days for the last little while,
>Starts with Hope.
>And,

Clarity. Confidence. Compassion. Love. Curiosity.
Then the mind gets bored.

>Or maybe it doesn't know what to do with
those feelings.

>(They feel too foreign.)
>As time goes on,

I can feel Hope being chipped away by
>Thoughts.

Like tiny splinters off of a block of ice.

>(Of ice because I know how to assemble
the pieces back together, but they melt away as soon
as my warm finger gets close.)

And something about the night time really wakes
them up.

>Is everything I do just a distraction?
>This sort of feels like making sense
>(of it).

I'm still not sure of anything at all though.
Except,

>I haven't felt so alone since my last
>depression.

But,

please don't pity me. It's understanding I seek.

All we want is love. And to love in return.

This feels too much a part of me to imagine being rid of it. How could anyone bear me this way?

> (Yet some how each day starts with

> Hope)

It's difficult to hear praise,

and that people seem to care.

I feel like I've done nothing that's worthy of any of it.

> (What the fuck is wrong with me?)

It's this cycle of thoughts, played on a loop.

Over another loop. And another loop.

Until all that's there is a clusterfuck of reality.

It feels like work to sleep at night. And I'm always clocking out early.

> (Jesus Christ what I'd do for a single day without this)

If this writing is confusing, it's because I'm confused.

How can I feel so god damn hopeful and equally lonely all at the same time?

I know it's not sadness. Or anger or guilt.

It feels like absolutely nothing then suddenly everything.

I know my worth. But I can't help but question it.

Because I go to bed alone. Feeling unworthy of love.

It's hard to imagine ever being able to accept love.

When that's all I want with all my aching heart.

Will I ever know it?

Here's to hoping tomorrow starts with Hope.

You Are

The white fluffy snow pacts down tight with each new footstep. I can feel the crunching of the snow up my legs. It's the only sound for miles. The air is dense with stillness and silence. I imagine tossing a branch in the air and watch it get caught in the density. Floating there, perfectly still against the vastness of the sky, looking like the first piece of a puzzle. All the trees are dusted with snow. They've been out here for decades. I wonder if they know I'm here too. Do they look down at all? Or does their thirst for the sun keep them staring up? (Lost in thought) Suddenly I see my breath, for the first time all year. The cold on my fingers, toes, and nose remind me I am in this body. This is aliveness. Signs of life, every single second of the day. You don't need to do (anything) to be alive. You are.

Clouded Judgment

A woven blanket of clouds stretch the distance of the sky.
There's an end to it somewhere, but in the moment I'm
staring at infinity.
Not even the Sun stands a chance some days at being con-
sumed.
How I miss the warmth of light now that everything feels
cold.

(And everything is grey now, too)

I've lost track of the days I've wished for clear skies,
only to find my head in the clouds.
The sensation of floating. The view from up here,
can feel intense like no other.
But the cloud is just a kaleidoscope.
And I am more than a cloud.
But damn, what power a cloud holds while holding noth-
ing at all.

Fear is a Monolith

Perpetually at the edge of a cliff,
my heart constanly pounds as if I'm eternally
falling.
(my feet create their own gravity to the
Earth)

My fate can only be reached beyond the cliff,
yet I find myself looking back towards
land.
(it's what I know)

Both views have their own beauty,
but the possibility of new beauty only lies
beyond the horizon.
(at least I think)

It's surprising I haven't bored myself with this cycle.
It's been 32 years.
(and I'm prone to boredom from time to time)

"A running start is all I need, then let go."
But every step seems to stomp gravity out in all direc-
tions.
(then I'm stuck)

I push with all my strength, trying to break free.
The audacity of me, to think I can defy gravity.
(the pressure is too much)

I've thought of repelling. And every other scenario. Anything
other than the answer I'm avoiding. To give in to the force. Let
it pummel me into a speck of dust. Then even smaller than that.
Until I come out the other side anew. Wherever that is. The cliff
is Fear, and it's a monolith. It's time to let go.
But wait...

Here Comes the Ivy Again

I am an abandoned home consumed by ivy and weeds.
Hidden in plain sight, yet I rarely feel seen.
All the windows where light used to shine in their beams,
are now boarded up.

No light can come in, and I can't let light out.
This home is mine, but I feel trapped with myself.
I can't figure this out.
Some people come near, every now and then.
But if I can't be a home for myself, what chance do I stand?

When someone new comes close I feel the ivy retreat,
maybe this time they'll notice my white flag in defeat,
But they just take pictures. Look around at what once was.
Seems like this is what everyone does.

I'm never what they're looking for.
At least for no longer than a moment.
I want to finally end this cycle of torment.
If I can't be a home for even myself, what chance do I stand
of housing anyone else?
And here comes the ivy again.

All the cracks of old floor boards. All the shifting brick.
Begging for ears to hear I exist.
Sometimes our eyes meet, as I peek through the cracks.
But they just come and go. They never look back.
And here comes the ivy again.

Hills of Healing

"The world doesn't revolve around you", but it always feels like spinning inside of my head. It's hard enough to find my footing when I can barely find a clear thought. And when I finally feel I made it to the top of that mountain, a fog rolls in thicker than it has before. The path up that I left behind disappears before my eyes. With no clear way down, any wrong step feels like it could be my last. The wind howls as there's a storm closing in. It sends me tumbling to the bottom where my ego is waiting with a mirror, exposing my cuts and bruises.The rain from the storm pours down and washes away the blood and masks the tears that cover my face. With my unhealed bruises I make the climb again tomorrow and hope for no fog. Cause one day there'll be no fog. Right? And bruises heal. Right? I'll use the scars that remain as a reminder that I've made it to the top before.

Nourishment

What delectable vibrations. Highs and lows. And combinations of the two. Infinite combinations of the two. Resonating in the hallows of my ears. Eliciting the firing of synapses in the valleys of my brain. Coursing through my blood into the valves of my heart. Pumping. Filling and emptying in the space in my lungs. Such delectable vibrations that make my skin tingle. Passing through the hairs on my arms and up the back of my neck. Chills. I'm carried through all of existence in every new moment that appears. Here. And here. And then. Time does not pass, but I am taken somewhere. Taken by the delectable vibrations. I have yet to find anything else like you. Cherished in every cell of my being. I vibrate with you. How delectable I feel. How delectable you make me feel.

Radiate and Reshape

My feet sink into the sand.
We become one.
Are we not a pile of sand?
Are we not made up of a million particles being shaped and eroded by time and people and nature?
I sit in you and close my eyes.
My body disappears and I imagine what it feels like to be you.
I feel the warmth that you feel. Radiating.
I hear the waves of the water crashing all around, the sound coming from all directions.
Wind blowing loose parts of you away, reshaping every second.
You are never the same thing.

You cling to parts of me, an enticing beg to stay.
You remind me that we are not separate.
I'll carry you back and show you other parts of me.
Reshaped. I left loose parts of me behind to be washed away and strewn about.
I don't need those anymore, and I hope it's an adequate reciprocation of the parts of you I left with.

Kiss Me Before Midnight

"Kiss me before midnight."
I'll kiss you in the light of day.
So I can see the glow of your face.

I move in slow.
Taking you in.
Before the moment takes us both.

I'll kiss you before midnight.
And after too.
And for all the time I didn't know you.

We're as close as we can get.
And we kiss. (Before midnight.)
The moment taking us both.

To a place where time has no truth.
Not a truth like this.
Not a truth like kissing you.

All the Borings in Between

Let me share my world with you
& not just the exciting parts,
but all the borings in-between.
I want true intimacy.

I want to show you my slow Monday morning.
When I play love music for myself while I put away the laundry
& finally wash all the dishes
& make myself lunch.

I want you to see all of the minutes I spend meditating
& the rarest occasions when I feel free enough to dance on my own
& when I laugh out loud
& all the spoonfuls of guiltless ice cream.

I've never shown myself this much love before.
Yet somehow I still can't fully accept it.
I want you to see all the ways I reject myself,
so that you can also see me never giving up.

This is the best I can do right now.

I Will Make Time for You

I will make time for you

When your body is weak and sore and tired,
I will make time for you.
When you feel full of grief and sadness,
I will not hide it away, I will make time for you.
When you are missing connection to people,
I will make time for you.
When you're bursting with happiness and affection and love,
I will make time for you.
When the world is too loud and the quiet is what you need,
I will make time for you.
I can not make time for the time that I let go by with no intention
to make time for you,
but now, today, and for the rest of forever
I will make time for you.

Trust Your Intution

I felt my body let go,
and suddenly I knew it was the right decision.
I could finally enjoy cutting a watermelon again.
A gentle smile.

The Look of Desperate Permission

I've never seen eyes scream help like that before.
So tired. So much suffering. So ready.
The look was of desperate permission.
Yet through every labored breath,
you still made time to pray for me.
And all of us.
And when I held your hand,
years of unexpressed love flooded my body,
finding its way out through my eyes.
Your face looked different.
Your voice so hoarse,
as if each breath carried away pieces of you with it.
Even in those moments you'd drift away to try and rest,
your body seemed to use every muscle at once to take the
next breath.
And the next. No rest at all.
I hope that you can find that final breath that will bring
you peace.
And when I'm struggling, I hope to find the breath that
brings me peace.
And brings me the strength you left for us.

To be human is so fragile, though we pretend we aren't in that
time between birth and death.
We hide behind jobs, homes, and identities.
All we have is the now. Even this very moment is gone. I'm tired
of chasing peace where it doesn't exist; back then or sometime
ahead. I'm okay, now. I'm everything I need to be, right now.

Welcome Home

I am from always, and from all over too.
Home is right now, but from then and tomorrow too.
I've been there before, and it looks like today.
But today resembles some other place.

I have no shape.
I flex and bend. And pulse and shift.
This form I am is a hologram.
Have you seen never?
We're surrounded by never.
And by always. All at once.

Right now becomes then in an instant.
And even quicker then has come and gone.
You're from there too.
Welcome home.
I've been waiting.

To W.W. (pt.1)

I feel most myself when I speak in cadence. Words delivered in dance. The word-dance penetrates the soul. I now understand the 'naming of songs', for our souls sing to one another. Sharing love and ideas separated by time. Though the words are still, they dance. Though the ink silent, it sings. Our songs. Their songs. The songs of the time. Of our time. Of their time. Time and life have no end when we put them to song and dance.

To W.W. (pt.2)

Your love for love, how do I love like thee? For I'd love to love like thee. Do I look outward or inward? Do I look at all? Should I close my eyes and smell or taste? Or is it the sound of ambience I seek? Perhaps my doubts of love have dulled my senses. This I refuse to believe, for I feel the love you have for all. How do I love like thee? For I'd love to love like thee.

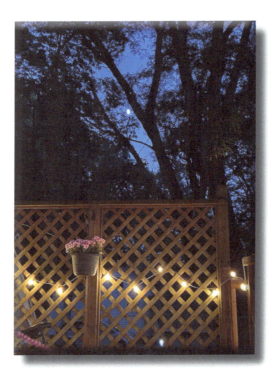

"My ears deafen with the cries of others. Through time and space and distant lands. Reaching all of those also alone."

- dsiii

The Cicadas' Summer Song

The trees burn fierce with the fire of the Sun.
Their trunks a pulsing orange like the logs of a well kept fire.
I stare, waiting for them to set ablaze.

Cicadas singing the Sun to bed with their unison'd lullabies.
The crickets wait patiently for their parts.
I feel like I'm listening to an orchestra warm up.

(An orchestra with no visible conductor, but a palpable presence leads with such precision)

The trees hold strong as the Sun stands no chance against the songs.
The cicadas silencing themselves one by one.
And now the crickets take the lead.

The mosquitos get bored and come out for a snack.
They could probably smell the fresh melon in my blood.

This night is just like every other,
and there's nothing wrong with that.
Because once I discovered this show,
I wait for it like clockwork with the rest of them.

And we all become a little more alive, as we bid the Sun goodnight.
The crickets continue their elaborate song,
as we welcome the Moon for the encore.
(We only have her for a couple more weeks.)

This is the best show on Earth.
Have you seen it?

We Sat for a Moment Longer

She shines bright in between the stripes of thin grey clouds.
How modest she can be.
All the shades of black and grey,
yet it's all so full and vibrant.
There is no darkness when she is around.

I no longer forget about you in the shadow of the Sun.
(I eagerly await your appearance)
I always make sure to look for you.
I always make sure to greet you.
And acknowledge your vibrance...

(As the last piece is cloud cleared away:
"Oh, that breeze feels good."
The wind stopped)

…Suddenly the clouds cleared as I finished my sentiments,
and the wind gently blew, but just for a second.
A cool touch on my face and in my body,
as if to extend her vibrance in reciprocation.
"I'm glad I came out to see you," I say back.

We sat for a moment longer.

Will You Stay, and Sway with Me?

Will you stay, and sway with me?

Let us sway together, to the sounds of it all.
All the chirps and creaks and cracks.
I hear music all around. Will you listen to the songs with
me?

(Speaking is optional.)

Either way, I want to feel your skin touch mine. I want touch
and movement to say what we can't. All the things we've
held back, from ourselves and each other and those we miss.
Even the ones we have trouble forgiving. I want to feel what
the music does to your body.

And maybe you'll feel what it does to mine, too. And to my
heart and my soul. These are the moments that I want to
share. These are the moments that make us a part of the
song. A part of it all.

Will you listen to the songs with me?
Will you sway with me to the sounds of it all?

*"I never thought the world owed me anything,
but it felt like it was depriving me of everything."*

- dsiii

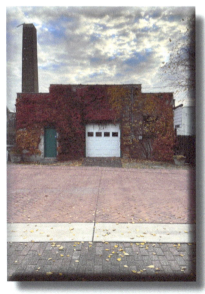

"The only thing I'll miss about our time together is the sunsets."

- dsiii

"I'll always forgive. And I'll always love you. And it might always hurt to. But that's okay.
I say that with such certainty this time."

- dsiii

The Truth of a Mirror

We take pictures of ourselves, cause we hate the truth of a mirror.
Or maybe it's to feel alive.
I know I take pictures of myself to remember I'm alive, but it's because I don't trust a mirror.
The reflection of me is a projection, and at times, I'm convinced I'm not really here.
We make up truth in our minds, and I'm scared one day I'll see my truth.
(If I'm not here, where am I?)

What do I even look like at all?
I might as well be a smeared painting,
found in the corner of a dusty room.
Home to the local spider.
Some people like that look, I suppose.

I spend my days begging to be noticed.
A reminder that I'm alive.
I hate that I need such reassurance.
It's just that, I feel like I've been here before, and I'm so bored with it.
I feel like I've been everywhere, and nothing's exciting anymore.

Time happens in all directions, and I feel the pull and push stronger than the Earth's gravity.
Memories might as well be today.
And right now is already yesterday.
Tick. Tick. Tick.

I hate that I'm always waiting to be found.
(by someone)
It's as if I'm traveling through time, longing for something I lost.
Whilst having no clue what that might be.

You lose yourself, when your constantly looking.
You forget that you're even here, always trying to be at the next possibility.
(And the next)
Maybe that's why we take pictures. To map where we've been. Or to make up our own version.
Because we hate the truth of a mirror.

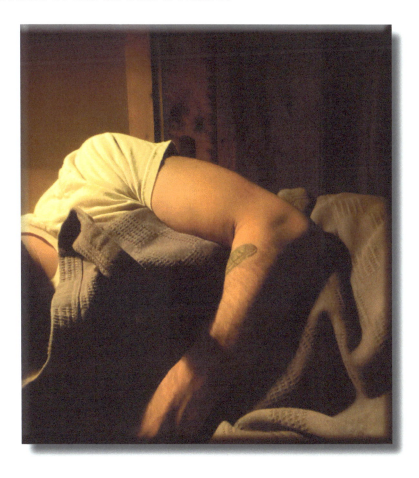

"Just looking for somewhere to belong. Will I ever find it here? It feels like I'm just passing through. Just looking for someone to share with. Will I ever find it here? It feels like everyone is just passing through (me). It's only true until it's not. I'll just pass through until then. There's still everything to come."

- dsiii

Thank You

- dsiii -

Milton Keynes UK
Ingram Content Group UK Ltd.
UKHW050244291223
435090UK00002B/4